They've Played for Timelessness
(with Chips of When)

David Breeden

VIRTUAL ARTISTS COLLECTIVE
http://vacpoetry.org
ISBN: 978-0-944048-11-5

Cover and interior image by Debby Sou Vai Keng, used by permission:
http://vacpoetry.org/debbysouvaikeng

Cover design by Regina Schroeder: http://forgetgutenberg.com

The title of this book is from a poem by ee Cummings, "Death(having lost)

"Blessing Joseph" and "Chaplain, On the Road from the Hospital" first appeared in *Journal of Pastoral Care & Counseling.* "Falling into the Sky (Based on a Poem by Zen Monk Muso Soseki)" first appeared in *Blue Lyra Review.* "Fido for the Hell of It" and "Lion a Lot like You" first appeared in *Poetry Superhighway.* "Killing the White Spider" and "The Usual Apologies" first appeared in *The Lit Journal.* "Meditation, God's Name" and "Meditation, Not Fallen" first appeared in *The Eloquent Atheist.* "Riff on Ortega Y Gasset" first appeared *Whiskey Island Magazine.* "Seeing" first appeared in *Bosporus Art Project Quarterly.* "Shipping Out" first appeared in *Driftless.* "Staining the Day" first appeared in *On the No Road Way to Tomorrow: Poems from the Chicago-Kunming Poetry Group.* "They Came With Expectations (Mark 16)" *Good News, Easter Issue 2011,* a publication of the Unitarian Universalist Christian Fellowship. "Written on Realizing my Father has Dementia" first appeared in *Sangam.* "Young Person: Your Life" and "Yeats Said That" first appeared in *Lady Jane Miscellany.*

Many of these poems first appeared on Tumblr: http://revdocdavid.tumblr.com/ and Twitter, @dbreeden

For my son Patrick, poet and artist.

Contents

I.

Breathe in
Breathe out

This teaches
How it is—

We take—
We give

With What Knows Who (Genesis 32)

Happens after the night
Wrestling with the dark
With what knows who—

Wrestling the place;
Wrestling the time;
Wrestling the matter;

Wrestling until dawn
Calls shadow home,
The dark and the light

That never fight about it.
And sometimes a sacred wound,
Jacob to Israel,

Displaced and un-named,
One other into a thing.
Happens after a night

Wrestling with
What knows who.

Bobbing on Surfaces

Because of your bother
with the surfaces,

the old masters say,
you have lost what is basic,

what is bright,
what is wonderful
about your own mind.

You have covered it,
losing it like a coin.

And so it feels as if
you are on a wheel

going round;
and so it feels

like treading water
in an endless sea.

Find, right now,
the old masters say,

your own
bright mind.

Meister Eckhart Said Somewhere

We fight the dark
not knowing that
the knower
and the known
are one. Confused

people imagine—
Meister Eckhart, mystic,
said this somewhere—
confused people see
the sacred as if it stood
over there and we here.

And so it is
we fight the dark,
thinking and thinking
that the sacred is there,

not here.
Meister Eckhart said,
the sacred and I—
(which means the sacred
and you and . . .)

we are—the sacred and us—we are
one in knowledge.

My Covenant with All That Is

I pledge to follow
the earth's gentle curve
as I go;

I pledge to breathe only air as I am able;
I pledge to breathe often;

I pledge to eat of the earth;
nothing other shall pass my lips.

I pledge to wend along the ways,
trodding earth, never air,
clouds and sun above,
what rocks are there under foot.

I pledge to see as best I can in bright sun;
I pledge to squint as I am able in dark;

I pledge to remain
upright at times
when I am able;

to lie prone when the need arises.

I pledge to find flames hot;
to find snow cold;
to find water according to its fashion;

I pledge to love as best I can;
to hate sparingly;
to mock seldom;
to judge not;

to jump to few conclusions;
to subscribe to few illusions.

I pledge to be
as I am able
and to cease
as the rules require.

Chaplain, On the Road from the Hospital

Riding home on the bus
I read David Hume on miracles
Empiricism nailing superstition
(As it does every time, good
Cop grilling the bad guy)

Riding home on the bus
Twenty-four hours at the hospital
Holding a mother
As life drained from her son
His one yellowed eye searching

The ceiling as she asked
"He knows I'm here, doesn't he?"
He knows I'm here. . ."
And the smile on the face
Of a girl I met retching in her bed

A smile after just a touch
Of holy water and a smile
On the face of a man whose arm
The doctors had ruined
A smile after a prayer

No—there are no miracles
Hume is right—there are none
Except for the death of reason
In the wonder of eternal dust

Blessing Joseph

Joseph on suicide watch
Dying of kidney failure
Shaking in his bed
Afraid to go back
To the nursing home
"Don't send me back
To that place"

I lay my hand on his forehead
Pray until he quiets
Come back an hour later
He whispering, shaking
"Do that thing
Do that thing where
You put your hand on my head"

Joseph, out of a gang
In a bed, shaking
Semi-quadriplegic, gnarled
Scars across his chest
Talks in a whisper
Shaking, twenty-four
In bed forever

Giant birds tattooed
On his chest heave under
The weight of bullet holes
"Do that thing
Do that thing where
You put your hand on my head"

Doom's Integration
(based on the writing of Sufi master Llewellyn Vaughan-Lee)

1.

Plunge in, you
have no choice—

Moses and Khidr meet
where the waters meet
and dead fish
come to life
and living fish
do the other.

There was no "I"
to tell this story.
There never is.

One sea is divine mind,
the other human.
There was no "I"
to tell this story.

There never is.

World of nothingness,
world of forms,
light, darkness,
love without self,
the I telling the story,

the I not.

The place
two seas
meet—There
there can be no "I"
telling this story.

Borders lost,
mystery found,

Elijah and Khidr
meet every year
where the waters meet;
there is no "I" there
to tell that story.

There never was.

Moses, Elijah, and Khidr
gather like the two seas
and the living fish,
and the dead fish to speak,

But there is no there
there to tell the story.
never was there an "I."

The fish, the dead
and those going
the other way,
ask, Why is it,
why is it,
divine purpose
plays the stages
in living form?

There was no "I"
to tell that story.

Moses, Elijah, Khidr
gather with the two seas
and the living fish,
and the dead fish to know

that when we part
from time to infinite,

when we dissolve
into love
eventually, there
is no I there, yet

for now, for here,
the purpose
is the flesh
and its doings
and an I to tell.

Until we dissolve
into love we
must speak
in the flesh where
the two seas meet
and the fish. . .

where the unbound
and the I meet, and
the dead fish become
alive and the alive fish
the other. Go ahead,

plunge in—You have

no choice . . .

2.

So many ways to be lost,
so many to be found;
so many paths to purpose
where the two seas meet,
the bound and not.

Moses, Elijah, and Khidr
gather like the two seas
and the living fish,
and the dead fish to speak,
the divine purpose
into human form.

There is no I there
to tell those stories.
There are no stories
that have no I.

Moses, Elijah, Khidr
the seas and the fish
resolve, dissolve,
solve.
Into story.

"Be!" says Khidr.
"Be!" says Elijah.
"Be!" says Moses
and the fish

in chorus,
be, be, and be
says the two seas
into the I not there,
and the story
that can't be told.
Plunge in, you

have no choice

II.

Words are a door—
Come inside;

Falling into the Sky

(based on a poem by Zen Monk Muso Soseki)

Years end ways
I dug and dug

Deeper into the earth

Looking for blue heaven
Choking always

On piles of dust rising

Then once
At midnight
I slipped

And fell into the sky

Jehovah Jireh (Genesis 22: 1-12)

And it came to pass
that God did test Abraham,
and said unto him: "Abraham,"
and Abraham, patriarch,
madman, said: "Here am I."

For God then apparently
knew not where
everyone was . .

"Take now thy son,
thine only son
(for you do have others
But some don't count
all that much),
whom thou lovest,
even Isaac, that son,
and get thee to Moriah;
and offer him there
for a burnt-offering
upon one of the mountains
which I will tell thee of."

For God then apparently
spoke like that
or leastways apparently
humans heard like that;

And this is a story of obedience;
and this is a story of obsession;
and this is a story

that makes little sense
aside from those mad for fervor.

And Abraham took the wood
and laid it upon the back
of Isaac his son to carry;
for the low
do the carrying,
and Abraham took in his hand the fire
and the knife
for the high
carry the stuff for killing;
and they went
both of them together.

For you must then
kill your pretty ones;
it is an obsession and
drives artists like God
mad.

And Abraham stretched forth his hand,
and took the knife to slay his son.
For God then apparently
had given us neither
firing squad,
chairs electric,
chambers of gas, nor
lethal injection
and so asked for knifings.
And the angel of the LORD
out of heaven

called to that wretched father,
saying, "Abraham, Abraham."
And he said: "Here am I."
And that angel up there said:
"Lay not thy hand upon the lad,
neither do thou any thing unto him;
for now I know that thou art
a God-fearing man, seeing
thou hast not withheld thy son,
even thine only son,
at least the only one that really
matters, from Me."

For God then
didn't know
the hearts of men,
how we do dream of killing
all our pretty ones . . .

No,

apparently not.

Monologue Overheard

'Use to be'
Them's the magic words

You use to be
A exotic dancer
I use to be
Mean to you

Them's the magic
Words—use to

Be—ain't no more

Them's the magic words

After Zen Master Hsu Yun

Here's truth for you—
saints are like everybody else.
Everybody else.

Finding a difference is like
buying a ticket
when you wrote the play.

Every truth thrives
in a human heart.
It rains, the flowers perk up.

After you see what the lies are
you will paint with all
the colors of life and death.

Saints are like everybody else.
Everybody else.

Yeats Said That

sometimes I know
the poems they

fall in crevices
never to squirm
never to speak

sometimes I know
the lyrics they

are a feather
dropped in
a canyon

yes, I wait

and wait
for the echo

Lion a Lot Like You

lion leaping into
the cedar blue air
only concrete but
fierce enough to tear
imagination to shreds

lion leaping from
ivy encroaching
lion escaping
a gothic perch
lion leaping
never moving

lion snarling
at a thought
snarling at a thought
that made him fierce
but froze him in concrete

The Usual Apologies

Trophies pulled from cars—
Eyeglasses, binoculars
A Lugar, bayonet, buttons
Gold fillings in a matchbox
A watch on a chain

My father and uncles out
Under the shade trees
After Sunday dinner, beer
And cigarettes, they talked
Until it sounded logical

—I got this off
A dead Jap—This
Off a dead German
They talked until it
Sounded logical

Until they became
Old men as dead
As the young men
They'd killed

Where I Come From

the night
in the country I come from
is bigger than anyone—

a thing itself
that will break all
persistent enough
to embrace it

the night
where I come from
holds animal and ghost

and a darkness
that could be either
and might be both

it breaks all
persistent enough
to embrace it

the night
in the country I come from
drives us to fire

which may save us when
we do not leave it
for the embrace

of the night
in the country
we all come from

III.

Concepts are a threshold—
Step over;

The Hand-Off

I remember the
XXth Century
strangely enough

& threshers
in the fields
& pieces of

uniforms still
on the farmers
turned from soldiers

(but never did we
beat our swords
into plowshares

never did we
share for all that

never did we
cease studying war)
I remember the
XXth Century

strangely enough
& the farmers
turned to dust

raising the future
like bales of hay
too heavy—Here

take this to
another century
destroyed

All in the Shuddering Now

Smell of an orange
seizes the day,
an airplane cabin
on a Monday.
When we know our story

is not the only one,
nor even ours;

when we know
at last the terrible
beauty that ours

is the only story,
the shuddering weave
of an orange that passed—
pillar to post,
tree to eaten

to enjoyed—
and never ours
but always us all.

Riff on Ortega y Gasset

The philosopher said,
I am I plus my surroundings.
The philosopher said,
If I do not preserve the latter,
I do not preserve myself.

The philosopher said,
I am I
Plus what
Is around me,

And if I do not
Preserve that
I do not preserve
Myself.

The philosopher said,
I am
I and what
Surrounds
Me. If I do not
Save that

I do not
Save myself.

The philosopher said,
I am not alone.

The philosopher said,
I am
What surrounds me:

If I do not preserve all,
I do not preserve
Myself.

Truth-Telling Does

Cuts the words
to the bone,
truth-telling does;

cuts the time spent
into stone,
truth-telling does;

burns the words
deep to deep,
truth-telling does;

like lake,
like clouds,
truth-telling does.

To wade in the sky
cuts to the bone,
truth-telling does;

to words, to riddles,
truth-telling does;
cuts the words

to bone,
truth
does.

Killing the White Spider

Letting go is not an easy thing
It's dark clouds in drought
And so wanting rain
It's a bus trip at night, no signs

It's dark clouds in drought
Waiting for rain, getting darkness
It's a bus trip at night, no signs
Wandering where and where

Waiting for rain, getting darkness
Wandering where and where
And so wanting rain
Letting go is not an easy thing

Written on Realizing my Father has Dementia

We are the flames that rise
Tongues of flames that rise
For a little, little while

For a few, few moments
Rising in wind
We are the flames warm

That dance a while
Call into the night
Gingerly, tenderly

Cracking for awhile
And we are the embers
The embers blown away

Staining the Day

Black butterfly drawn by my white paint
Flutters, flutters, her movements bred
To beat the birds, to cross the fields

Why does she want my paint?
I wave her away

Is it the unnatural white?
The sweet chemical smell?

What does she see, this butterfly?
What is it this creature of flowers smells?

I wave my brush at her
Busy in my barn painting
Busy to get done and on

She waves
She flutters
She goes back to flowers

I go back to spattering
The newspapers beneath my feet
With fine rains of drops
Hoping to write some
Hoping past this work

She comes back
The white, the smell
I don't know
Yet she dives, somersaults in
Black in a pool of chemical white

Hopelessly bound and lost
In the tar in the smell ***no stanza break
Only her legs free
I flick her out onto the newspaper
A poor, folded thing herself

Only her legs and head
Anything but white
Gone
Dead
Only a question of time
And it's up to me
To turn away
Or stop the suffering

I stomp, hard
Onto the grotesque origami
A bit of pink spills out

Flower or brains or blood
Whatever it is
It stains the paint
It stains the paper
It stains the day

Fido For the Hell of It

A black Lab who'll
Answer to any name
Has wandered up
To the farm. He goes

Along with me on
Long winter walks
I call him Fido

For the hell of it
We walk into morning
Frost that sparks like
A carpet of diamonds

"Fido" I say just
For the hell of it
"Are we more than
The names we give?"

He wags his tail. Nothing
Has a name here but
For us for a while

We walk into evening
Fields blued by solstice's
Cold, trees bared but
For a slight mist rising

Shipping Out

She's looking forward
to spring, really she is
after all this cold. She
has the seed catalogue
open just to prove it

which reminds her
which reminds her
of how her husband
dead these two years
you understand

how he loved asparagus
which is just like the time
back during the war
when they lived in that place
place close to the base

and he was always about
to ship out, you understand
so they went ahead
and got married
and her mother really didn't mind

really she understood
and her dad did too really
how things were then
and that spring, always
about to ship out

and the garden—how he
loved to garden and

he thought he would die
over there and loved to garden
back when he was alive

do you wanna see
wanna see his picture?
she says, looking forward
to spring, really she is
after all this cold

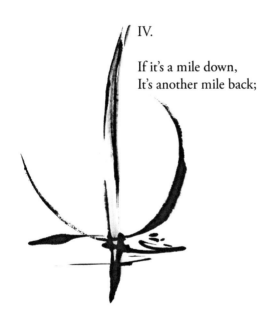

IV.

If it's a mile down,
It's another mile back;

Stoning Honi (63 BCE)

Honi the Circle-
Drawer could
Pray down rain;

Could talk to God,
Who would listen.
"Pray for us!"

Said one side.
"No, for us!"
Cried another.

"God doesn't take
Sides, you petulant,
Evil children!"

Honi said as
He died
Under stones.

Flesh Remembering

I

When I crawl through catacombs
Gathering dust that must be bones

I'm thinking I'm thinking
I'm thinking it is
The flesh that's always

Remembering

II.

When I crawl through catacombs
Gathering dust that must be bones

I'm thinking I'm thinking
I'm thinking I'm
Remembering

Is flesh always

III.

When I crawl through catacombs
Gathering dust that must be bones

I'm thinking the dust
Must be bones

Remembering

The flesh must be
Bones remembering

When I crawl
Through catacombs

After Chiao Jan, Monk

How is it
We talk the end

Before we hit the shore?

It is the rowing—

Autumn wind
Hard

On the water.

Turning Around

Looking back can kill you.
Ask
Lot's wife;
ask
Orpheus
the harp player—

can kill you—

sometimes stone dead,
pillar of salt stiff;
sometimes despair,
but cold;

ask the harp player
torn out of song;

ask the woman
whose only name
is "Lot's wife;"
ask . . .

and there are other
ways
to turn in darkness,

to look back,
done by even more
anonymous we's.

Ask the guy
With the harp.

Young Person: Your Life

Gather lore;
Remake the wheel;

And next . . .
And then . . .

•

Seeing

like the ceiling for the sick
staring too long
blemishes and patterns

forming into things
St Bernards jumping clouds
minotaurs drinking beer

staring too long
and patterns appear
cryptomorphs from chaos

patterns and patterns
designs in the mind
only in the mind

Close Shave

didn't know I'd come this way
so long after
the Burma Shave signs had gone

like so much
just accident

even the Jesus
is Coming Soon!
sign has bleached
in the sun into
yellowed haze

I did not know then
what a blue road was

though the moss
on shingled shed roofs
might have been a clue

like a larvae weaving
Its cocoon I
struggled, bending

like the puling drunk
so often I was
building, building

Now I find myself here
on the way again
and only those things

built way before me
for landmark—

Here are your struggles

Just look at 'em stretch

Think you might beat this?

You're caught in the catch!

Burma Shave

Meditation, God's Name

God is not God's name
Allah is not Allah's name
Yahweh is not Yahweh's name

Elohim is not Elohim's name
Brahman is not Brahman's name
Mazda is not Mazda's name

Reason is not reason's name
Truth is not truth's name
Multitude is not multitude's name

Names are not names
Naming is not naming
Naming names nothing

Meditation, Not Fallen

We are not angels fallen
We are apes rising
We are not descended

To violence but
Rising to peace
We are not fallen

We are not angels
We are apes rising
When we rise

We are not fallen
Except in choosing
Not to rise

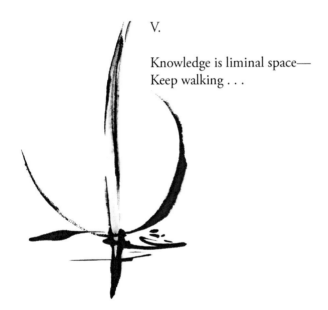

V.

Knowledge is liminal space—
Keep walking . . .

No Saying

(an adaptation from Zen Monk Royokan)

No path leads to awakening;
no path leads to a destination;

when we see a glimmer of awakening
and head straight for it,
we find that it recedes and recedes.

when we seek truth with our heads,
even when we find good ethics,
we have taken the wrong path.

I cannot say how my path is;
when I describe it, it falls to pieces.

Compassion
(an adaptation from Zen Monk Royokan)

The wind has stilled
But still flowers fall

And birds sing, though
Silence lies at the heart

Of each song. Yes, no—
Mystery—cannot be

Known or found, only
The virtue of Compassion.

The Problem with Trophies
(an adaptation from Chuang Tzu)

When the archer merely shoots,
all his skill is there.
when he shoots in a contest,
he gets nervous.

When he shoots for a trophy,
he goes blind
or sees double—
he loses his mind.

His skill has not changed,
but competition
divides his thoughts—
he thinks of winning,
not shooting;

desire takes away his skill.

If the Shoe Fits
(an adaptation from Chuang Tzu)

Chu'i the draftsman
drew circles freehand
more perfect
than any compass.

He drew off the cuff,
his mind free and unruffled.
He took no thought—
he let concepts go
and encountered no blocks.

When the shoe fits,
the foot is forgotten;
when the belt fits,
the waist is forgotten;
when the mind relaxes,
bad and good disappear.

When worries are forgotten,
the self is free—
no obsessions, no compulsions,
no repulsions, no attractions.

When the beginning is right,
the end is simple.

Forget the correct way;
forget that the way is easy.

Running, Running
(an adaptation from Chuang Tzu)

Once there was man
afraid of his shadow
annoyed by
the sound of his footsteps.

He decided to
run from both.

Yet when he ran,
down went his foot,
and there was a footstep

and his shadow followed
and followed.

The man said,
"It's only that I'm not
running fast enough!"

And so he ran, and ran,
faster and faster.

He ran and ran
until he fell dead.

Now: what, do you suppose,
might have happened if
the man had stopped
and rested in some shade?

Traps
(an adaptation from Chuang Tzu)

We use a net to catch fish;
after we catch the fish,
we drop the net.

We use words to say ideas;
after we say the ideas,
we should drop the words.

Yet where is someone
who has dropped words?

We need to talk!

We're Born There

(an adaptation from Chuang Tzu)

Fish are born in water,
we are born whole.

If fish seek in water,
they find all they need.

If we do not seek
in anger and worry,

we find all we need.

The Taoist

(an adaptation from Chuang Tzu)

The Taoist acts without stops,
harming nothing,
yet never thinking about
compassion.

The Taoist does not work at gain
yet does not value poverty.

The Taoist acts without stops,
self-reliant,
yet with no pride
in going it alone.

The Taoist stays anonymous.
Virtue is its own reward.
No self is the self.
The greatest person is nobody.

Suddenly In My Office
(Adapted from Zen Monk Chao-pien)

with no thoughts
I sat in my office

my mind like still water
until thunder knocked
the door open

and there sat
my homely old mind

VI.

C'mon

Don't be a
Wallflower

At the dance
Of the cosmos

Walking Into

I walk in purple clover
away from the task at hand,
which is—as usual—

sorting the past into
what to burn
and what to box;

I walk in poison ivy
with the task at hand,
which is—as usual—

what to trash
and what to crate
into tomorrow;

I walk in sunlight
into the task at hand,
which is—as usual—

the only direction—
purple clover, poison ivy,
which are sunlight.

Elegy for Kevin Joe Eldridge

Just saw you died
fellow traveler out
of the hillbilly dark
of Southern Illinois

cancer it appears
and I suppose
it was the cigarettes
you looked so
suave smoking

It isn't the mortality
pulls me up but
missing your life
so caught in mine

and

now that time
has slowed so
that old men
might talk, you're
gone back to
the hayfields

out to map the
country we dreamed
must be somewhere

Keep writing poems
there fellow traveler
into the hillbilly dark

The Problem of Suffering

last time I
spoke with God I
asked about
just that problem

and got an earful—

when you create
everything

some things are
going to slip through—

you know,
like suffering,
like death

things like that

Our Brother Billy Died Bilingual

(the last words of Billy the Kid)

"¿Quien es?
¿Quien es?"
Billy the Kid
May have said

Last words,
July 14, 1881--
"Who is it?
Who is it?

Pat Garret
Or some
Real assassin?

Who is?
Who is?

Was the question
Is
Meta-physical
Ultra-physical

Cri de animales
O cri de la ages?

Brother Billy was

Then bullet
Then was not

So it was with
Our brother Billy

Gathered here
In line for the boat
In line for the plane
Gather with me here

Lista, lista
¿Quien es?"
¿Quien es?"
Billy may have asked

Cri de cour
Cri de
Cri of

Oh, you will...
Too

"¿Quien es?
¿Quien es?"

Muy mysterioso

They Came with Expectations (Mark 16)

They came to the tomb,
Those women—Mary, and
Mary, and Salome—worried,

Worried about the weight
Of the stone. They came
With intentions; plans. They

Came with death in mind;
They came with assumptions.
They found life instead—

Mary, and Mary, and Salome.
"Where is he?"
They asked a young man

Dressed all in white.
"Where is he?"
"He's not here."

"But where is he?"
"He's not here."
"But where is he?"

"You see where he was."
"But where is he?"
"He's not here."

"Where is he?"
"He has risen."
"Where is he?"

"He went
Before you
Into Galilee."

The women—Mary, and Mary,
And Salome—came worried,
Though at least they came.

They came, expecting the dead.
Where is he?
He has gone before you.

When and When It Is the Morning of the World

When you know your point
of view is a blind spot;

when your this is your that;
when your yes and your no
lope off, caressing;

when your here is as well as your there;
when your good is just as bad;

when your opposites
aren't any more;

when you know you are sitting
on the limb you are sawing off
like any animated character;

when you watch yes and no romp
off your leash without shouting;

when the flags of inevitable armies
are the stuff of dreaming;

when all the words
of all the prophets

are so many warbles in the song;
when your dance is where you rest serene . . .

open those other eyes;
look—
it is the morning of the world.

About the Author

David Breeden has an MFA from The Writers' Workshop at the
University of Iowa, a Ph.D. from the Center for Writers at the
University of Southern Mississippi, with additional study at
Breadloaf and in writing and Buddhism at Naropa Institute in
Boulder, Colorado. He also has a Master of Divinity from Meadville
Lombard Theological School in Chicago.

His poetry, essays, and short fiction have appeared in such journals
as *Mississippi Review, Nebo, Poet Lore, Mid-American Review,
North Atlantic Review, Boston Literary Review, Turnstile, Nidus,*
and *Paragraph.* He has published four novels and twelve books of
poetry. He is on the editorial board of Virtual Artists Collective.

His book *This Is Just To Say: Variations on a Theme of William
Carlos Williams* was nominated for a Pushcart Prize and the Award
in Religion and The Arts from the American Academy of Religion.
His book *News from the Kingdom of God: Meditations on The
Gospel of Thomas* recently appeared from Wipf and Stock
Publishers. His book *Raging for the Exit,* a collaborative work with
Steven Schroeder, is forthcoming.

Breeden is a Unitarian Universalist parish minister in Minnesota.

CPSIA information can be obtained at www.ICGtesting.com
Printed in the USA
BVOW041519250612

293455BV00001BA/1/P